CREDIT TO WEALTH IN 30 DAYS

HOW TO BUILD FINANCIAL FREEDOM USING CREDIT, BUSINESS, AND INVESTING

DUANE YOUNGBLOOD

Elevate Your Life with Duane

TABLE OF CONTENTS

INTRODUCTION

THE TRUTH ABOUT WEALTH NOBODY TOLD YOU

"Hard work can make you a living...
but understanding creates
wealth."

DUANETHESUCCESSKING

Let me tell you something most people will never say out loud...

Hard work does not build wealth.

Now don't get me wrong—hard work matters. But if hard work alone created wealth, the hardest working people would all be rich. They're not.

I know this because I lived it. I was working hard... doing what I was told... trying to be who people needed me to be. And while I was doing all of that, I was losing myself—and I was losing financially.

At the same time.

I had moments where I looked successful. I had access. I had opportunities. But I didn't have understanding.

And without understanding, access becomes a trap.

The Moment That Changed Everything

That's what happened to me with credit. I got my first credit cards in college with no training, no guidance, and no real plan. I did what most people do—I spent. I enjoyed the moment. I felt like I was winning.

But I wasn't winning. I was being trained.

Trained to use money the wrong way. Trained to react instead of think. Trained to look successful without actually being successful.

And before I knew it, I had destroyed my credit... and I didn't even understand how.

But that moment changed everything. Because instead of staying stuck, I made a decision. I was going to learn the system. Not just use it... not just survive it... but understand it so well that I could win with it.

And that decision took me on a journey.

What This Book Is Really About

A journey through Credit. Business. Investing. Failure. Growth. And most importantly... identity.

Because here is what I discovered:

You don't build wealth with money first. You build wealth with understanding. And once your understanding changes... your actions change. Once your actions change... your results change.

That's the pattern.

Believe → Feel → Act → Detach

When you believe differently, you feel differently. When you feel differently, you act differently. And when you act differently... your life changes.

This book is not just about credit. It's about alignment. Credit. Business. Life. Because when those three are aligned... money flows. When they are not... life feels like a struggle no matter how hard you work.

Both Sides of the Story

I've lived both sides. I've been confused, off track, trying to please people, building a life that didn't fit me. And I've also been clear, focused, aligned, walking in purpose.

And I can tell you this with certainty… there is a path to wealth. Not a guess. Not luck. Not hope. A path.

And that path runs through understanding credit, building business, and using money to make money. That's what this book will show you. Not theory. Not motivation only. Strategy. Real strategy that you can use.

What You Must Decide Before We Go Deeper

But I need you to understand something before we go further… this only works if you decide to walk your path. Not your family's path. Not your friends' path. Not the path people expect from you. Your path.

Because wealth is not just money. Wealth is peace. Clarity. Freedom. Time. Alignment.

And if you follow what's in this book, you won't just make more money… you will become someone who knows how to keep it, grow it, and use it to change your life—and your family's future.

So as you read… don't just read to understand. Read to apply. Read to shift. Read to become.

Because if you do… you are not just reading a book. You are stepping into a new life.

Be Blessed

Duane Youngblood

CHAPTER 1

THE POWER OF A JOURNEY

*"You don't need to know where you're going…
you just need to stop standing still."*

DUANETHESUCCESSKING

I remember standing in a place where everything in my life looked right... but something inside me knew it wasn't.

Have you ever been there? Doing what you're supposed to do... following the plan... making people proud... but deep down, something just doesn't feel right.

That was me.

The Plan That Got Changed

I had a plan. A clear one. I was going to leave Pennsylvania and go to Oral Roberts University to study accounting. I was ready to go. Ready to grow. Ready to become something more.

Then life stepped in. My father lost his job. And just like that, my plan was gone. I was told I had to stay home. Find a local school. Adjust.

So I did what many people do... I adjusted my life to fit the situation. I enrolled at Duquesne University. It wasn't what I planned—but it was what I had.

Now here's where it gets interesting. At the same time, I got accepted into a program called INROADS. That program connected me with an internship at Westinghouse Electric. So while I felt like I had lost something... I was actually gaining something.

I was traveling. Meeting powerful people. Learning things most people my age had never been exposed to. On the outside... I was winning. But inside... I was still searching.

The Moment That Changed Everything

When I got on campus, something caught my attention immediately. Credit card applications were everywhere. Tables. Flyers. People signing up like it was nothing.

I was 17 at the time, so I couldn't apply yet. But I watched. And I waited.

Three months later, I turned 18. And I did what everyone else was doing. I applied. Not for one... not for two... but for four credit cards. And I got approved.

That moment felt like power. I could buy what I wanted. Go where I wanted. Look like I was doing well.

But let me tell you something... looking successful and being successful are not the same thing.

The Trap

No one taught me how credit worked. There were no conversations at home about money. No lessons about responsibility. No understanding of what I had just stepp-ed into.

So I did what most people do when they don't understand something powerful... I misused it.

I charged. I spent. I lived in the moment.

And within nine months... I was late. Over the limit. Getting calls I didn't want to answer.

And here's the truth most people won't admit... I didn't just not know what to do. I didn't want to deal with it. I avoided it. Because when you don't understand something… avoidance feels easier than responsibility.

But avoidance has a cost. And I was paying it.

The Wake-Up Call

I went from feeling like I had access… to realizing I was trapped. I had destroyed my credit before I even understood what credit was. And that's when something shifted in me.

I made a decision. Not to run. Not to hide. But to learn.

I decided I was going to understand the system. Not just use it. Not just survive it. But master it.

That decision took me on an 18-month journey of studying credit laws, consumer rights, and financial systems. And what I discovered changed everything. There were rules. There were systems. There were ways to win.

But most people lose for one simple reason… they never learn the rules.

The Real Lesson

See, my journey wasn't just about credit. It was about something deeper. It was about identity. Because I had to face something about myself: I liked the image of success… more than the responsibility of success.

And until that changed… nothing else would.

That's a hard thing to admit. But it was the truth. I wanted the look more than the work. I wanted the reward more than the discipline. And as long as I stayed in that mindset, I would keep building things that collapsed.

Maybe you can relate to that. Maybe you've been chasing the image instead of the foundation. Maybe you've been focused on what things look like instead of what they're built on.

That's not a judgment. That's a pattern. And patterns can be changed.

The Truth About the Journey

Here's what I need you to understand... a journey is not about knowing exactly where you're going. It's about having the courage to move... when you don't.

The dictionary says a journey is traveling somewhere. But 'somewhere' means unspecified. Unknown. Unclear. That's where most people get stuck. They won't move unless they can see the whole path.

But life doesn't work like that.

The people who win are not the people who had perfect plans. They're the people who kept moving when things got uncertain. They adjusted. They learned. They stayed in the game.

Believe → Feel → Act → Detach

Everything changed for me when I shifted how I approached life. I stopped waiting to feel ready. And I started choosing differently.

I believed I could understand. I began to feel capable. And I started acting with intention. And that's when things began to change.

What Your Journey Looks Like

Your journey is not going to look like mine. It shouldn't. Because you're not me. You have your own story. Your own starting point. Your own lessons to learn.

But the principles are the same.

Every successful person you admire went through a journey. They had moments of confusion. Moments of failure. Moments where quitting made more sense than continuing.

But they stayed. They learned. They grew.

And now you're reading about them.

Your journey is not the problem. Your journey is the path. And if you stay on it… learn from it… grow through it… it will take you exactly where you're meant to be.

Final Thought

Your journey may not look perfect right now. It may feel unclear. Uncomfortable. Even painful.

But don't miss this… the journey is not the obstacle. The journey is the teacher.

And if you let it teach you… you will become someone who doesn't just survive the road ahead. You will become someone who knows how to lead others down it.

CHAPTER 2

WHY FINANCIAL JOURNEYS ARE NECESSARY

*"Money doesn't change your life—
your direction does. And direction always
requires a journey."*

DUANETHESUCCESSKING

I once met a man who made good money. On paper… he looked successful. Nice car. Good job. Always busy. But one day, we had a real conversation.

And he said something I'll never forget. He said, 'Every month I start over.'

That stuck with me. Because from the outside, he looked like he was moving forward… but in reality, he was running in place.

Have you ever felt like that? Like no matter how much you make… how hard you work… how much effort you put in… you're not really getting ahead?

That's not a money problem. That's a direction problem.

Busy… But Not Building

Most people are doing something every day. Working. Paying bills. Handling responsibilities. But doing something is not the same as building something.

That man wasn't lazy. He worked hard. But everything he did was temporary. His money came in… and went right back out. Nothing stayed. Nothing grew. Nothing multiplied.

And that's when I realized something powerful… if your life is not designed to build, it will be designed to survive.

Survival mode is exhausting. You're always catching up. Always one problem away from being behind. Always working but never arriving.

And the sad part? Most people don't even know they're in it.

The Missing Piece

When I first started my journey, I thought money was the goal. Make more money... fix everything. That's what most people believe.

But I learned something the hard way... money doesn't fix a broken system. It exposes it.

If your habits are off... more money makes it worse. If your mindset is off... more money disappears faster. If your direction is unclear... more money just takes you further off track.

Think about that. The thing you've been chasing—more income—could actually make your situation worse if the foundation isn't right.

That's not a popular truth. But it's the truth.

What I Observed

After I went through my credit situation... I started paying attention. Not just to myself... but to other people. I saw something that didn't make sense at first.

People with less income were moving forward... while people with more income were stuck. Why? Because one group had direction... and the other only had income.

Direction without income is frustrating. But income without direction is dangerous. Because it gives you the feeling of progress while you're standing still.

The Truth Most People Avoid

Here's the truth most people don't want to hear... you don't need more money right now. You need a better path. Because without a path, you will spend what you make, repeat what you've always done, and stay where you are.

Not because you're not capable... but because you're not positioned.

Positioning is everything. Where you stand determines what you can reach. And right now, the financial journey is what repositions you.

Why the Journey Matters

A financial journey forces you to face things most people avoid. It makes you look at your habits, your decisions, your patterns, your beliefs.

And that's uncomfortable. But it's necessary. Because you can't change what you won't face.

I had to face the fact that I was emotional about money. I made decisions based on how I felt in the moment, not where I was trying to go. I had to face the fact that I was avoiding hard conversations—with myself, and with others.

That was painful. But facing it was the beginning of freedom.

The Pattern Behind the Problem

Most people try to fix money on the surface. They budget. They cut back. They try to 'do better.' But they never go deeper. They don't look at why they spend the way they do. They don't question what they believe about money. They don't change how they think.

So nothing really changes.

The surface looks a little better for a few weeks. Then life happens. And the old patterns come back.

That's not failure. That's what happens when the root hasn't been dealt with.

Believe → Feel → Act → Detach

Every result in your life follows a pattern. What you believe shapes how you feel. How you feel drives how you act. And how you act creates your results.

If you believe money is hard to keep... you will feel pressure. If you feel pressure... you will make emotional decisions. And emotional decisions rarely build wealth.

But when you believe that wealth is a skill... you feel curious instead of anxious. And curiosity leads to learning. Learning leads to better decisions. Better decisions lead to better results.

From Survival to Strategy

Most people live in survival mode. They react to life. Bills come, they respond. Problems show up, they react. But people who build wealth move differently. They operate with strategy. They think ahead. They plan. They position themselves.

And that doesn't happen by accident. It happens through the journey.

The journey is what forces you to stop reacting and start creating. It's what shifts you from victim to architect. From passenger to driver.

You're Not Behind

Now let me say something to you directly... if you feel like you're behind, you're not. You're just at the beginning of awareness. And awareness is where everything changes.

Because once you see it... you can't unsee it.

That man I told you about? He wasn't stuck because he lacked effort. He was stuck because he lacked direction. And once you understand that... you gain power. Because direction is a choice.

And starting today... you get to choose a new one.

Final Thought

Your financial journey is not punishment. It's preparation. Every step you take on this path is building the version of you that can actually hold the wealth you're chasing.

Most people want the money before they're ready for it. The journey makes you ready.

So don't rush it. Don't skip it. Embrace it. And watch what happens when you do.

CHAPTER 3

CREDIT

"Credit is not the problem... lack of understanding is. Learn the rules, and the game changes."

DUANETHESUCCESSKING

At 18 years old… I thought I had just stepped into freedom. I remember holding those credit cards in my hand like they meant something. Like I had made it. Like I was finally in the game.

No cash? No problem. Want something? Just swipe. Need something? It's right there. It felt easy. Too easy.

And that's the part nobody explains.

The Illusion of Power

See, credit looks like power when you don't understand it. You can buy now. You can move faster. You can live ahead of your current situation.

But what I didn't know at the time was this… access without understanding is a trap.

I wasn't using credit. Credit was using me.

And the worst part? I felt good about it. I felt powerful. That feeling masked what was actually happening. I was building debt, damaging my future, and stepping into a hole I didn't even know was there.

What Nobody Told Me

No one sat me down and said: 'Here's how this works. Here's how you win. Here's how you lose.'

There were no rules given to me. Just approval. And approval feels like validation when you're young. So I did what most people do… I followed my feelings instead of a plan.

The fast fall was predictable—in hindsight. At first, nothing felt wrong. I made purchases. Minimum payments. Kept going. But then things started to change. Balances got higher. Payments got tighter. Stress started to build.

And then it happened. Late payments. Over-the-limit fees. Collection calls.

In less than a year... I went from feeling powerful... to feeling stuck.

The Truth I Had to Face

Here's the hard truth I had to accept: it wasn't the credit cards. It was me. Not because I was irresponsible... but because I was uneducated. And there's a difference.

Irresponsible means you knew and didn't care. Uneducated means you never had a chance to know. I was uneducated. And once I accepted that, I stopped feeling shame... and started seeking knowledge.

That shift—from shame to curiosity—was everything.

The System I Didn't Understand

Once I made the decision to learn, everything changed. I started digging into how credit actually works. And what I found shocked me. There was a system. A real system. And it wasn't complicated... it was just hidden.

I learned that credit is tracked, behavior is recorded, and patterns are rewarded or punished. Everything you do with credit sends a signal.

Your payment history tells lenders if you can be trusted. Your balances tell them if you're in control. The age of your accounts tells them how long you've been managing credit. Every single action leaves a mark.

The Shift

When I understood that... I stopped seeing credit as money. And started seeing it as a tool. A tool that could either build my future or destroy my options.

And that's when everything changed.

I started treating every credit decision like an investment. I asked: does this help me or hurt me? Does this send the right signal or the wrong one? Is this building trust or breaking it?

Those questions changed my behavior completely.

The 4 Things Most People Miss

Most people use credit every day... but don't understand the basics that control everything. They don't understand when their balance is reported, how their usage affects their score, why timing matters, or how lenders actually evaluate them.

So they keep doing what feels right... and getting results that don't make sense.

Here's what you need to know:

First—balance reporting. Your balance is typically reported to the credit bureaus around your statement closing date. Not your payment due date. That means if you carry a high balance when your statement closes, that's what lenders see—even if you pay it off right after.

Second—utilization. If your credit limit is $1,000 and you're carrying $800, that's 80% utilization. That's hurting you. The goal is to stay below 30%, and ideally below 10%, when your balance is reported.

Third—consistency. One great month doesn't rebuild years of damage. But 12 consistent months starts turning the ship. It's not one grand gesture—it's steady, disciplined behavior over time.

Fourth—lender evaluation. Lenders don't just look at your score. They look at your profile. How long have you had credit? How diverse is it? What type of accounts do you have? A high score with a thin profile can still get denied.

The Real Purpose of Credit

Credit was never designed for you to live on. It was designed to evaluate you. To measure how you manage money, how consistent you are, how disciplined you can be. It's a report card. Not a paycheck.

Once you understand that, you start playing the game differently. You stop using credit to fill gaps in your income. You start using it to build a track record that opens doors.

The Identity Problem

Here's where it goes deeper. Most people don't have a credit problem... they have an identity problem. They see credit as a way to survive, a way to get by, a way to cover gaps. Instead of a way to build, a way to position, a way to create opportunity.

And until that identity shifts… nothing else will.

Your credit is a reflection of how you see yourself. If you see yourself as someone who struggles, you'll manage credit like someone who struggles. If you see yourself as a builder, you'll manage credit like a builder.

Believe → Feel → Act → Detach

If you believe credit is confusing and unfair… you will feel frustrated. If you feel frustrated… you will act inconsistently. And inconsistency destroys credit.

But if you believe credit is a learnable system with clear rules… you will feel empowered. And when you feel empowered, you act with strategy. Strategy builds credit. Built credit builds opportunity.

What Credit Can Really Do

When used correctly, credit can open doors, lower your costs, give you access to capital, help you build business, and position you for wealth.

I've used credit to fund business operations, cover strategic expenses, and access capital at rates most people never see—because I understood how to position myself to receive those opportunities.

That's not luck. That's strategy.

Final Thought

At 18, I thought credit was freedom. Now I know the truth. Credit is a tool. And like any tool… if you don't understand it, it can hurt you. But if you learn it… it can build a life most people only dream about.

You're not stuck. You're just in the learning phase. And learning is where power begins.

CHAPTER 4

BUSINESS

"You're already building something every day… the only question is—does it belong to you or someone else?"

DUANETHESUCCESSKING

I worked hard for years. Showed up on time. Did what I was supposed to do. Handled my responsibilities. From the outside... it looked right.

But one day, something hit me. Everything I was building... didn't belong to me.

Have you ever had that moment? Where you realize you're giving your time... your energy... your focus... to something that won't stay with you?

That moment changed how I saw work forever.

The Wake-Up Realization

I wasn't lazy. I wasn't doing anything wrong. I was just building the wrong thing. I was helping someone else grow... while my own life stayed in the same place.

And that's when I understood something simple—but powerful: if you don't build your own system, you will spend your life supporting someone else's.

That's not a knock on employment. Employment has its place. But employment alone cannot give you freedom. It gives you income. And income and freedom are not the same thing.

The Trap Most People Don't See

We're taught early in life: go to school, get a job, work hard, be responsible. And there's nothing wrong with that. But here's what's missing... no one teaches you how to own.

So people spend years becoming great workers... but never become owners. And ownership is where everything changes.

When you own something, it can work for you. When you work for someone else, you are the machine. And machines don't get days off. They don't get equity. They don't get to step back and watch the system run without them.

Business ownership is how you become the system instead of a part of it.

The Shift From Worker to Builder

When I started learning about business, I didn't have everything figured out. I didn't have all the answers. But I had something more important... awareness.

I realized: a job pays you once. A business can pay you again and again. A job gives you income. A business gives you leverage. And leverage is what creates freedom.

That awareness changed everything. Because once you see that distinction, going back to the old way of thinking is almost impossible.

It Didn't Start Perfect

Let me be real with you... my journey into business wasn't smooth. There were mistakes. There were wrong decisions. There were moments I questioned everything.

I've launched things that didn't work. I've invested in ideas that didn't pan out. I've hired people I shouldn't have and passed on opportunities I should have taken.

But every step taught me something. And every lesson moved me forward. Because business is not about perfection... it's about progress.

The entrepreneur who wins is not the one who never fails. It's the one who learns faster than they fail.

What Business Really Is

Most people think business is about having a big idea, making a lot of money, or being your own boss. But that's not the full picture.

Business is about solving problems. That's it. When you solve problems... people pay you. When you solve bigger problems... you get paid more.

Every successful business in history is built on one thing: identifying a problem that people have, and making their life better by solving it. The more people you solve it for, the bigger the business.

That's it. Strip away everything else, and that's what it comes down to.

The Connection to Credit

Now let's connect this to what we talked about before. Credit gives you access. Business gives you purpose for that access.

Without business... most people use credit to survive. With business... you can use credit to build. That's a different game entirely.

When I secured business credit lines, I wasn't buying things to feel good. I was investing in inventory, marketing, tools, and infrastructure that generated returns. That's credit working for you instead of against you.

Credit plus business strategy equals access to capital that can compound your growth. That's not theory—that's what happens when both systems are aligned.

The Difference Between Spending and Building

Before business, most people use money for bills, wants, and temporary needs. But once you step into business... money becomes a tool. You start asking different questions.

Will this help me grow? Will this create more income? Will this move me forward? That shift alone changes everything.

I remember the first time I made a business purchase and knew—with certainty—that the money would come back multiplied. That feeling is indescribable. It's the difference between consuming and creating.

The Identity Shift

Here's where it really changes. You stop seeing yourself as someone who works for money... and start seeing yourself as someone who creates money. That's an identity shift. And once that shifts… your behavior follows.

Believe → Feel → Act → Detach

If you believe you're just a worker… you will feel limited. If you feel limited… you will act small. But if you believe you are a builder… you begin to feel capable. And when you feel capable… you take bigger, smarter actions.

And bigger, smarter actions build bigger results.

Structure Matters

One thing most new entrepreneurs overlook is business structure. How you set up your business legally affects everything—your taxes, your liability, your ability to get funding.

An LLC, S-Corp, or C-Corp is not just paperwork. It's a signal to the financial world that you're serious. It separates your personal finances from your business finances. That separation is critical when it comes time to access business credit and funding.

Many entrepreneurs never get funded simply because they never properly structured their business. They're still operating like a side hustle instead of a company. And lenders treat it that way.

Structure your business like a real business—because it is one.

Final Thought

That moment I realized I was building something that wasn't mine... was one of the most important moments of my life. Because it woke me up. And once you wake up... you can't go back to sleep.

Start asking today: what am I building? Because that question changes everything.

CHAPTER 5

INVESTING

"Money grows when you stop spending it and start positioning it."

DUANETHESUCCESSKING

I watched people make money… and lose it just as fast. Paychecks came in. Bills got paid. A little was spent here… a little there… and before they knew it, it was gone.

Then I saw something different. I saw someone who didn't rush to spend their money. They paused. They thought. And instead of spending it… they placed it somewhere. And over time… that money grew.

That moment changed how I saw everything.

The Question That Changed Me

I started asking myself a simple question: what if my money could work… the same way I do?

Because up until that point… I was working for money. But money wasn't working for me.

That's the fundamental difference between the wealthy and everyone else. The wealthy have money working on their behalf—around the clock, even while they sleep. Everyone else trades time for dollars and wonders why the finish line never gets closer.

The Trap Most People Stay In

Most people live in a cycle: work, get paid, spend, start over. And they repeat that cycle for years. Not because they want to… but because they don't know another way.

No one teaches investing in school. No one sits you down and says, 'Put something aside so it can compound.' You're taught to earn and spend. And if you're lucky, maybe save a little. But saving is not the same as investing.

Saving keeps money. Investing grows money. The difference is positioning.

My First Real Understanding

When I began learning about investing, I realized something powerful: money is not just for spending. It's for positioning. Where you place your money determines what it does next.

If you spend it... it's gone. If you position it... it can grow. That sounds simple. But most people have never thought about money this way.

Every dollar you earn has a destination. The question is whether you're choosing that destination intentionally—or whether it just goes wherever it wants.

It Wasn't About Being Rich

Let me be clear... I didn't start investing because I was rich. I started because I wanted a different result. And that's important. Because many people think: 'I'll invest when I have more money.'

But the truth is... you build the habit before you build the wealth.

Warren Buffett started investing as a child. Not because he had a lot—but because he understood the principle early. You don't need a large amount to start. You need a consistent practice.

Small Moves... Big Results

At first, the amounts may feel small. But it's not about the amount. It's about the pattern. Because small, consistent actions over time... create big results. That's how investing works.

This is called compound growth. And it is the most powerful financial force available to everyday people. When you earn a return and reinvest that return, you begin growing not just on your original amount—but on everything that's been added.

The longer you let it run, the more powerful it becomes. Time is the ingredient that most people waste.

Understanding the Basics

You don't need to be an expert to start. You just need to understand a few key ideas.

First: money grows over time. If you let it sit in the right vehicle and don't touch it, it will be worth more later than it is today.

Second: consistency matters more than timing. You don't need to invest at the perfect moment. You need to invest regularly. People who try to time the market almost always lose to people who simply stay in the market.

Third: risk should be understood, not feared. Risk is not the enemy. Uninformed risk is the enemy. When you understand what you're investing in, risk becomes manageable.

Fourth: diversification protects you. Spreading investments across different assets means one bad move doesn't wipe everything out.

The Emotional Battle

Let's be honest... the hardest part of investing is not understanding it. It's controlling your emotions. Fear will tell you to stop. Doubt will tell you to wait. Impatience will tell you to quit. But discipline says: stay consistent.

The market will go up and down. That's expected. The people who panic and pull their money out during downturns are the ones who lock in losses. The people who stay the course are the ones who benefit when things recover—and they always recover.

Believe → Feel → Act → Detach

If you believe investing is too hard... you will feel unsure. If you feel unsure... you won't act. But if you believe investing is a path to growth... you will feel confident enough to start. And starting is what creates momentum.

Money With a Purpose

When you combine what we've talked about so far... everything begins to align. Credit gives you access. Business gives you income. Investing gives you growth. That's the system. That's how wealth is built.

Each element feeds the next. Credit funds the business. Business generates income. Income fuels investment. Investments grow and create passive income streams.

Passive income eventually replaces active income. And that's when you arrive at freedom.

Final Thought

I once saw money as something to use. Now I see it as something to place. And that difference... is what separates those who stay the same... from those who build something greater.

Start placing your money with intention. Even small amounts. Even imperfect amounts. Because the habit you build today will compound into the life you want tomorrow.

CHAPTER 6

TIME WEALTH

"If money costs you your time,
you didn't get rich—
you just got paid."

DUANETHESUCCESSKING

I remember being busy all day… moving from one thing to the next. Handling responsibilities. Checking things off the list. And at the end of the day… I felt exhausted.

But here's what bothered me the most… even after doing all of that… I still felt like I wasn't getting anywhere.

Have you ever felt like that? Like you're doing everything right… but something still feels off?

That was me.

The Moment That Opened My Eyes

One day, I stopped and asked myself a simple question: where is my time going?

Not my money. My time. Because I realized something I hadn't paid attention to before… I was spending my time the same way I used to spend my money. Without a real plan. Without intention. Without strategy.

And just like money without a plan disappears, time without a plan disappears too. The difference is you can earn more money. You cannot earn more time.

Busy… But Not Free

I had income. I had movement. I had things happening. But I didn't have freedom.

And that's when it hit me… you can be busy and still be stuck.

In fact, busyness can be one of the most dangerous traps for an entrepreneur. It gives you the feeling of progress without the results. You go to bed tired every night thinking you worked hard. But hard at what? And toward what?

Busyness without direction is just noise.

The Lie We're Told

We're taught that success looks like this: work more, do more, stay busy, keep going. And eventually... you'll make it.

But what they don't tell you is this... if your time is always controlled by something else, you're not free. No matter how much money you make.

I've met people earning six figures who are slaves to their calendar. Every hour is spoken for. Every day is someone else's. They've traded freedom for income. And most of them can't even see it.

The Trade Most People Don't See

Most people are making a trade every day... and they don't even realize it. They trade time for money, energy for income, life for a paycheck. And while that may work for a season... it was never meant to be permanent.

The goal was never to work until you die. The goal was to build until you no longer have to trade time for money.

That's the real finish line. Not retirement. Not a number in a bank account. The ability to choose how you spend your hours.

What Time Wealth Really Means

Time wealth is simple. It means you control your time. Not your job. Not your schedule. Not your circumstances. You.

It means you can choose when you work, how you work, and what you focus on. That's real wealth.

When I wake up in the morning and decide how my day looks—that's wealth. When I'm present for a family moment without guilt—that's wealth. When I can take a call or turn one down based on what matters—that's wealth.

None of that requires a specific dollar amount. It requires a system that gives you options.

The Shift From Money to Freedom

Before, I thought: 'If I just make more money… everything will be fine.' But I learned… more money without control of your time creates a different kind of stress. Because now you have more to maintain… but not more freedom.

Freedom is not a dollar amount. Freedom is what happens when your financial system no longer requires your constant presence to run.

Protecting Your Time Like an Asset

Once I understood the value of time, I started treating it the same way I treat money. I stopped giving it away carelessly. I stopped saying yes to everything. I started asking: does this serve my direction?

Time is a non-renewable resource. Once it's spent, it doesn't come back. Yet most people guard their money more fiercely than they guard their hours.

Flip that. Start protecting your time first. Money can be replaced. An hour at 11pm when your child wanted to show you something cannot.

The Connection to Everything Else

Credit gives you access. Business gives you income. Investing gives you growth. But time wealth... is what gives it all meaning.

Because what's the point of building wealth... if you don't have time to enjoy it?

I've seen wealthy people who were miserable because they were chained to the machine that created their wealth. That's not the goal. The goal is alignment—where your Credit, Business, and Life work together so that you live well, not just earn well.

Believe → Feel → Act → Detach

If you believe time doesn't matter... you will feel comforttable wasting it. If you feel comfortable... you will act without intention. But if you believe your time is valuable... you begin to feel protective of it. And when you feel that you act with purpose.

Final Thought

I used to think success was about doing more. Now I understand... success is about having the freedom to choose less. To choose what matters. To choose how you live. To choose your time.

Build toward that. Every system you create, every investment you make, every credit strategy you execute—it should all point toward more freedom. That's the real destination.

CHAPTER 7

YOU ARE NEXT

*"Your life doesn't change when you get ready...
it changes when you decide you're next."*

DUANETHESUCCESSKING

I used to believe something that held me back for years. I believed success was for other people. People who started earlier. People who had more support. People who had better opportunities.

Not me. I didn't say it out loud... but I felt it. And what you feel... controls how you move.

The Quiet Lie

It's a quiet lie. One that sounds like: 'I'll get there one day.' 'I just need a little more time.' 'I'm not ready yet.'

But what it really means is... I don't see myself there yet.

And if you don't see yourself there... you won't move like someone who belongs there.

This is the most dangerous barrier to success. Not lack of money. Not lack of opportunity. Not lack of skills. It's a broken self-image that quietly keeps you anchored to where you are.

You can have every resource available to you and still not move—if you don't believe you deserve to.

The Moment That Changed Me

There came a moment in my life where I got tired. Not tired of working... tired of waiting. Tired of watching other people move forward... while I stood still.

And I asked myself a question that changed everything: why not me?

Not in a hopeful way... in a real way. Why not me?

That question did something powerful. It broke the pattern. Because for the first time... I stopped seeing success as something outside of me... and started seeing it as something I could step into.

You've Been Preparing

Let me tell you something clearly... you didn't go through everything you've been through for nothing. Every mistake. Every setback. Every moment of confusion. It wasn't wasted. It was preparation.

You were learning... even when it didn't feel like it. Growing... even when it didn't look like it.

Think about everything you've survived. Everything you've figured out. Every time you picked yourself up when you had every reason to stay down. That's not weakness. That's evidence of your capability.

You are more prepared than you think. You've just been comparing your behind-the-scenes to everyone else's highlight reel.

The Truth About Timing

Most people think they're late. Behind. Off track. Missed their moment. But that's not true.

You're not late... you're just now aware. And awareness is where everything begins.

Colonel Sanders started KFC at 65. Julia Child's career took off in her 50s. Samuel L. Jackson didn't break through until his 40s. Ray Kroc didn't franchise McDonald's until he was 52.

The idea that there's a deadline on success is a lie. Your window is open right now.

The Identity Barrier

Here's what really holds people back... it's not opportunity. It's identity. If you still see yourself as someone who struggles, someone who gets by, someone who hopes things change—then your actions will match that.

But when your identity shifts... everything shifts.

Your identity is not fixed. It's a story you've been telling yourself. And stories can be rewritten. Every chapter of your life is an opportunity to introduce a new version of who you are.

The question is: who do you choose to be from this point forward?

Believe → Feel → Act → Detach

If you believe 'I'm not ready'... you will feel uncertain. If you feel uncertain... you will hesitate. But if you believe 'I am next'... you begin to feel different. More confident. More willing. More open. And that feeling creates new action.

You Don't Need Permission

One of the biggest things I had to learn was this... I didn't need permission. Not from people. Not from my past. Not from my situation.

I could choose. And so can you.

Stop waiting for someone to tell you it's your time. Stop waiting for the perfect moment. Stop waiting until you feel ready. Ready is a feeling that comes after you act—not before.

What Happens When You Decide

When you truly decide... something shifts inside of you. You stop looking for excuses. You stop waiting for perfect conditions. You stop holding back. And you start moving. Even if it's small... it's forward.

That forward motion creates momentum. Momentum creates evidence. Evidence builds belief. And belief fuels the next action. It's a cycle—but it starts with a single decision.

Your Life Is Waiting on You

Let me say this directly to you... the life you want is not waiting on time. It's waiting on you. Waiting on your decision. Waiting on your belief. Waiting on your action.

This is your moment. Not tomorrow. Not next year. Now.

Because moments don't announce themselves. They show up quietly... and you either step into them... or you let them pass.

Final Thought

I spent years thinking I wasn't ready. Years waiting for the right time. But the truth is… the right time doesn't come. You create it. And when I finally understood that… everything changed.

You are next. Not eventually. Now. Step in.

CHAPTER 8

THE CREDIT STRATEGY

"Winning with credit isn't about having more cards... it's about having a plan."

DUANETHESUCCESSKING

I saw something early on that didn't make sense. People with good income were getting denied… and people with less were getting approved.

At first, I thought it was unfair. But the more I looked… the more I realized something simple: it wasn't about how much money they made. It was about how they were positioned.

The Difference Between Guessing and Knowing

Most people use credit like this: they guess. They swipe. They pay when they can. They hope things work out. But hope is not a strategy. And guessing creates problems.

If you're guessing with credit, you're leaving your financial future to chance. And chance is not a plan you want to bet your life on.

The people who win with credit are not the people with the highest incomes. They're the people who understand the system—and play it deliberately.

My Turning Point

When I decided to truly learn credit… I stopped guessing. I started studying patterns. What works. What doesn't. What lenders actually look for. And what I found changed everything.

There are rules to this. Clear rules. And once you understand them… you stop losing. You start winning. Every time.

Credit Is a Game... With Rules

Let me simplify it for you. Credit is a system that tracks behavior. It looks at how you use your accounts, when you make your payments, and how consistent you are. And based on that... it decides your level of trust.

That's it. There's no mystery. There's no luck. There's no favoritism. It's math based on behavior. And when you understand the behavior the system rewards... you can produce those behaviors on purpose.

The Real Goal

Most people think the goal is a high score. It's not. The goal is approval. Because a high score without the right profile... still gets denied. But the right profile... gets approved.

I've seen people with 780 scores get denied for business loans because their profile was thin. I've seen people with 680 scores get approved for significant funding because their profile told the right story.

The score matters. But the story matters more.

The Foundation of Strategy

Winning with credit comes down to a few key principles. Let me break them down simply.

1. Control Your Usage

Just because you have access doesn't mean you should use it all. High balances send the wrong signal. Low balances show control.

Keep your utilization below 30% on any single card and below 10% overall when your statements close. This one habit alone can move your score significantly over time.

2. Timing Matters

Most people don't realize this... but when you pay matters just as much as if you pay. There is a moment when your activity gets reported. And what shows at that moment... is what lenders see.

Pay your balances down before your statement closes—not just before your due date. Those are two different dates, and confusing them is a costly mistake.

3. Consistency Builds Trust

Credit is not built in one move. It's built over time. Consistent, on-time behavior creates strong results. One late payment can hurt. But 24 months of clean, consistent behavior can transform your profile.

Think of it like a reputation. Reputations aren't built in a day. They're built through repeated, reliable actions over time.

4. One Card Can Lead

You don't need to use everything at once. In fact... using one account the right way is more powerful than using many the wrong way.

Pick one primary card. Use it for regular purchases. Pay it down before the statement closes. Do this consistently. Watch what happens to your score over 90 to 180 days.

The Business Credit Dimension

Now here's where strategy gets powerful. Everything we've talked about in credit applies to your personal profile. But there's a whole other system—business credit—that most people never access.

Business credit is separate from your personal credit. When built correctly, it allows you to access funding without your personal credit being the deciding factor. It creates a financial identity for your business that lenders evaluate on its own merit.

This is how businesses access lines of credit, equipment financing, and capital that individuals never qualify for on their own.

Building business credit requires a properly structured entity, business banking relationships, vendor accounts that report to business bureaus, and a track record of consistent behavior—just like personal credit.

Most people miss this entirely. And it's one of the biggest gaps between people who stay small and people who scale.

From Confusion to Control

Before I understood this... I felt like credit controlled me. Now... I control how I show up in the system. And that's what I want for you.

This is about moving from reactive to intentional. From victim of the system to master of it.

Believe → Feel → Act → Detach

If you believe credit is confusing... you will feel unsure. If you feel unsure... you will act inconsistently. But if you believe credit is a system you can learn... you will feel confident enough to apply strategy. And that creates results.

Credit + Business + Investing

Now let's bring everything together. Credit gives you access. Business gives you income. Investing gives you growth. But strategy... is what connects it all.

Without strategy, you can have all three and still lose. With strategy, even a modest start can compound into something significant.

The people I've helped go from no credit to six-figure funding didn't do it by accident. They followed a strategy. Step by step. Patiently and persistently. And the results proved that the system works when you work the system.

Final Thought

I used to think credit was complicated. Now I see it clearly. It's not complicated... it's just controlled.

And once you take control... everything changes. Your options expand. Your opportunities multiply. And you stop being managed by a system you don't understand.

Learn it. Master it. Use it to build.

CHAPTER 9

FINAL THOUGHTS

"This isn't the end of your journey…
this is the moment you finally take control of it."

DUANETHESUCCESSKING

I remember finishing something once... something I thought would change my life. I had put time into it. Energy into it. Focus into it. And when it was done... I waited. I expected something to feel different. But nothing changed.

And that's when I learned something I will never forget... finishing something doesn't change your life. Applying it does.

This Is Your Moment

You've read about the journey, direction, credit, business, investing, time, and strategy. You've seen the path. Now the question is simple: what will you do with it?

Most people will read something like this... feel inspired... and then go right back to what they were doing. Not because they don't want change... but because change requires action. And action requires decision.

The gap between knowing and doing is where most people live. They know what they should do... but they don't move. They wait. They hesitate. They second-guess. And life keeps moving without them.

You Already Have What You Need

Let me tell you something clearly... you don't need more information right now. You need movement. Because everything you need to start... you already have.

You have awareness. You have understanding. You have the principles. Now you need to take that first step. Even if it's imperfect. Even if you're scared. Even if you're not sure where it leads.

Step anyway. The path reveals itself to those who move—not to those who wait.

The Identity You Choose

From this point forward... you have a choice. You can go back to old habits, old thinking, old patterns. Or you can step into something new. A new way of thinking. A new way of moving. A new way of living.

Your identity shapes everything. What you believe about yourself determines your actions. Your actions determine your outcomes. Your outcomes determine your life.

Choose a new identity. Choose to see yourself as someone who understands credit, builds business, invests wisely, and lives with time freedom. That identity—fully embraced—will pull you forward even when motivation fades.

Believe → Feel → Act → Detach

This pattern has been with you the entire time. Now it's time to live it. Believe that change is possible for you. Feel what that future looks like. Act in alignment with it. Not once... but consistently.

And then detach from the outcome. Do the work. Trust the process. Let the results come on their timeline. Because they will come.

The CBL Wealth Blueprint in Action

Everything in this book comes back to one truth: Credit, Business, and Life must be aligned for wealth to flow.

Credit gives you access. Business gives you income. Life gives it meaning.

When these three are working together, something powerful happens. Money stops being something you chase and starts being something that flows toward you. Opportunities start appearing. Doors start opening. And the stress that used to define your relationship with money begins to lift.

That's not a fantasy. That's alignment. And alignment is achievable for anyone willing to do the work.

Your Responsibility

At some point... you have to take ownership. Not blame. Not excuses. Not waiting. Ownership.

Ownership means you accept full responsibility for where you are and full authority over where you're going. It means you stop looking for someone else to fix your credit, build your business, or create your freedom. You do it. With guidance, with support—but you do it.

Because ownership creates control. And control creates change.

What Happens Next

This is where your real journey begins. Not when you finish reading... but when you start applying.

Step one: take an honest look at your credit. Know your score. Understand what's helping and what's hurting. Make a plan.

Step two: look at your business structure. Do you have one? Is it set up correctly? Can it receive funding?

Step three: look at how you're using your money. Is it being spent or positioned?

Step four: look at your time. Is it being controlled by others or designed by you?

These four questions will show you exactly where to start. Pick the area that needs the most work—and begin there.

The Legacy You Leave

This is bigger than you. The way you live... the way you grow... the way you build... it affects the people around you. Your family. Your future. Your legacy.

Every person you know who struggles with money is struggling because no one showed them the way. When you learn this, you become the one who breaks that cycle. Not just for yourself—but for everyone who comes after you.

That's a calling worth answering.

Your Final Decision

So let me ask you one last question... who are you going to be after this? Not what you learned. Not what you read. But who you choose to become.

Because that choice—made right now, in this moment—is the most important financial decision you will ever make.

Final Thought

I once thought I needed more time... more knowledge... more preparation...

But I was wrong. What I needed... was to decide. And once I did... everything changed.

This is not the end of your journey... this is the moment you finally take control of it.

Be Blessed.

Duane Youngblood

DuanetheSuccessKing | BizStart Group Inc.

ABOUT THE AUTHOR

Duane Youngblood, known as The Success King, is the founder of BizStart Group Inc. and a trusted coach to thousands of entrepreneurs seeking financial freedom.

With over 37 years of experience and more than 8,700 people served, Duane has helped individuals improve their credit, build fundable businesses, and create real, lasting wealth.

Through his proven CBL Wealth Blueprint (Credit, Business, Life), he teaches a simple but powerful truth:

When your life is aligned… money flows.

www.ingramcontent.com/pod-product-compliance
Lightning Source LLC
LaVergne TN
LVHW011050110826
845149LV00015B/3441
9780988755772